Against My Dreams

An Immigrant's Story

Against My Dreams

An Immigrant's Story

poems by

Linda Strever

PAINTED SNAKE PRESS
Olympia, Washington

Against My Dreams: An Immigrant's Story
Copyright © 2013 by Linda Strever
All rights reserved

www.LindaStrever.com

ISBN 978-0-9896228-0-6

Library of Congress Control Number: 2013914874

Cover and book design by Debi Bodett
www.DebiBodett.com

Cover and author photos by Barry Troutman

Printed in the United States of America

First Edition
Published by Painted Snake Press
Olympia, Washington

Acknowledgments

"Waiting for Nothing" appeared in *Floating Bridge Review.*

"Against My Dreams" appeared in the Awards XII edition of *Nimrod: International Journal of Prose and Poetry.*

"Without God" appeared in *Iris: A Journal About Women.*

"The Piano," "The Linen Closet," "Eye," and "Longer Streams" appeared in *Stanza.*

Enduring thanks to:
The women in the Norse Home in Seattle who gave me their stories: Laura Franswog, Jennie Hartmann, and Thora Myrseth.

The staff and volunteers of the many *folkemuseums* I visited in southern Norway, who gave me their knowledge of and enthusiasm for Norwegian history and culture. I would thank you by name, except that when I was mugged on my return to the U.S., I lost all my notes.

The following people for their ideas and support along the way: Diane Bailey, Andrea Bone, Steven Cahill, Sydne Cogburn, Terri Cohlene, Ruth Dinerman, Howard Evans, Doris Faltys, Pamela Firth, Don Freas, Debbie Geer, Stephanie Gombos, Lee Graves, Karen Harding, Dan and Polly Harris, Devon Haynes, Brenda Kaulback, Flora and Christoph Kimmich, Myra Kogen, Justine Kolesko, Edith Konstalid, Joan Larkin, Joanne Lee, Lawrence and Josephine Mark, Eileen McGorry, Mark Melady, Carol Millette, Bev Morris, Joanne Osband, Jennifer Presnell, Darcie Richardson, Kay Ridgway, Bonnie Rose, Sarah Rosenblatt, Joan Schaeffer, Helmut Schardt, James Scully, Kate Severson, Deb Shea, Emily Van Kley, Sonja Wentz, Mary Williams, Tina Wood, and Bhakti Ziek.

The following people *in memoriam*: Vita Laumé, James Merritt, Lois Rivard, Shirley Thrasher, and my mother, Thelma Strever, for her patience and openness in responding to my endless questions and for her encouragement of all my adventures.

My family in Norway for their hospitality, generosity, and family stories and photographs: Gudrun Knutsen, Nora and Reidar Ristvedt and their daughter Liv, Else Marie Uleberg, Olav and Evy Uleberg and their son Frank, and especially Kari Uleberg *(in memoriam)*, who gave me so much.

Eido Frances Carney, Susan Christian, and June O'Brien for turning my head around about the business of publishing.

Jeanne Lohmann, Lucia Perillo, and Marjorie Power for reading the completed manuscript and offering their written responses.

My team: Debi Bodett and Dean Jones.

The group (formerly known as) the Tuesday night poets for giving every single one of these poems their attention, feedback, and support: Chris Dahl, Sandra Fisher, Jeanne Gordner, Carol Gordon, Lucia Perillo, Cynthia Pratt, and Kristel Rogers.

And my husband, Barry Troutman, for all his love, for his amazing photography, for being first reader and proofreader, for the meals, the groceries, the laundry, the ironing, the cleaning, the listening, and the sheer joy he takes in my work.

In memory of my cousin

Kari Uleberg
1925 - 2013

"Only the lost is ours forever." The words ran in her mind. She had known them all her life, as one knows a nursery rhyme. There were moments when she glimpsed a truth in them—one of those truths which have to pass from mouth to mouth as a trite saying, just as the trolls have to make themselves small when a peasant is to take them in his boat.

Sigrid Undset

from *Images in a Mirror*
translation by Arthur G. Chater

Contents

PART II: 1917-1939

PART III: 1941-1980

Preface

These poems are written in the voice of my grandmother, Gunnhild Olavsdatter Breland, the daughter of a man who refused to believe that the earth is round. Born in 1894 in Breland, a tiny farm district of about sixty people on the outskirts of a village called Åseral in the mountains of south-central Norway, she was named Gunnhild after her maternal grandmother and was the fifth of eight children. It was the tradition in those days to take one's family name from the name of the farm. "Breland" means "land of snow patches."

In 1913, just after her nineteenth birthday, my grandmother followed her older sister to America and settled in New York City, a remarkable contrast to the landscape of her childhood; she never saw Norway or her parents again. She knew no English when she arrived and had about a year of schooling in her lifetime, gained when the schoolmaster would make his annual rounds among farming districts carrying the schoolbooks on his back.

As an exploration of an immigrant's life that spanned the Twentieth Century, this is a piece of the American story. It's also the story of a particular family, dominated by secrets and silences, and the story of a particular woman, marginalized by gender, national origin, social class, and mental illness. I see her life as a series of losses and dividing forces, her nature as an odd mixture of sensitivity and harshness. My grandmother lived to be ninety-five and remained a mystery to me. My purpose in this book is to allow her to speak.

The Family

In 1887 Olav Ånundsson Breland (b. 1847)
married Else Olavsdatter Eikil (b. 1856).

Their children: Ingeborg (b. 1887)
                           Ånund (b. 1889)
                           Olav (b. 1890)
                           Gunnar (b. 1892)
                           Gunnhild (b. 1894)
                           Marit (b. 1896)
                           Gunnvor (b. 1898)
                           Jon (b. 1901)

My grandmother met Andrew Stensen (b. circa 1893)
in America in 1916, and they married in 1917.

Their children: Arthur (b. 1918)
                           Thelma (b. 1919)

In 1940 Thelma Stensen, my mother,
married Walter Strever (b. 1917).

Their children: David (b. 1945)
                           Linda (b. 1949)

Against
My
Dreams

An Immigrant's Story

PART I: 1904~1917

Farmhouse at Breland, known as *Der Nede*, "There Below"

Seated: Gunnhild's mother and father, Else Olavsdatter Eikil and Olav Ånundsson Breland

Standing: Gunnhild's younger brother, Jon, and younger sister, Gunnvor

680 West End Avenue at 93rd Street circa 1940

Gunnhild worked here as a live-in maid until her marriage in 1917

Courtesy of The New-York Historical Society, New York City

Without God

April 1904
Åseral, Norway

Marit and I went to the place of the Devil.
We said three words three times. Now God is gone
from this farm. Gone from even the holy place
by the lake where stones lie rounded
in sun. We went to the place of the Devil
and told no one. Three words three times
behind the barn where jagged rocks stand
silent as knives. If Papa knew what I said . . .

Marit is dead. I know by her hair, spread
over straw the way Agnes' hair floated
before she sank under the ice. Dark under ice
and God was not there. Agnes stayed a long time
without God, and when she came out, she was dead.
Her mother would not speak until spring.

At supper one night Ingeborg chattered to Mama
about the earth being round. Papa didn't speak
until morning, and then he cursed the schoolmaster.
If Papa knew my three words, he'd stop speaking
altogether. Once when he chopped the head
from a snake, its body curled as if it would strike.
He threw it behind the barn, the head and the body.
I went there to look, and went there again.

Each piece of straw, each hair has a shadow spun
black by some spider. Three days ago Marit's cheeks,
her throat were blood red. Mama sat bathing
her forehead. Two nights ago she breathed fire,
and Mama sat beside her til dawn. Yesterday
her skin was dull as paper, and Papa carried her
to the barn. Mama sat quiet then.

Marit walks at night behind the barn. Three words
three times. I think she comes into the house. I hear
the door handle turn. God cannot live in a box.
The box for the baby at Ljosland was smaller
than Mama's thread bin. That baby never saw God,
buried too soon to get its name in the church. A curse
to die with no name. Ashes to ashes, dust. Agnes' box
was pale. Three shovels of dirt, now grass grows.

Papa says on Saturday we'll take Marit to God.
Mama says I mustn't come in here til Papa finishes
the box. There is a time in the evening when the light
inside grows stronger than the light outside. Marit's hair
used to fly about her face. The kitchen window
casts a glow on the ground like a shadow.

One Body

August 1906
Åseral, Norway

The buzz of a fly can make me jump,
so deep is the quiet in the mountains.
The church is like that, too, one
dark-clad body breathing with one
breath, lulled by the minister's buzzing.
His words drone, slow and measured,
but suddenly his voice lifts up, beats
against the roof beams, and the whole
body sits straighter in their pews. I watch
the backs of their heads, breathe out
when they breathe in, and hear
my thoughts, small flies inside my skull.

I imagine jumping off a cliff, falling fast,
where even Jesus cannot save me.
I sit straighter and glance around, sure
that someone knows. The minister's eye
rests on me. If God can hear my thoughts,
then so can the Devil, and I see them
shoulder against shoulder pushing
each other with all their giant might.

Marit lies behind the church. We stand
at her grave, Papa stiff, the boys fidgeting,
Mama and the girls in tears. I stand
and look and wonder if God is in the dirt,
if Marit has thoughts, still as stumps. We
used to blurt the same words, laugh together
in surprise. She was always thinking.

Another Morning

June 1911
Åseral, Norway

Papa says we need rain. He looks to the sky
when he says it, then bows his head, waiting
for God's liquid voice. The line around the lake
where water used to lie is sharp and distinct.
Papa says soon snakes will come down
out of rocks to drink from what is left,
twisting the shore like roots of unseen trees.

Ingerid's letter talks of people—not kings
and queens—who have crystal lamps
hanging from their ceilings, carpets
on their floors. August came back last year
to bury his father. He has climbed marble
stairways—in the day they are mirrors, reflecting
the sky in washes of blue, and at night
they shine like falls of light. Ingeborg's eyes
grow wild when she hears about America.

This morning I will prod the cows
to the upper pasture, sit with my sewing
and eye them. Hours later I will poke them
down for milking. Each day is like every
other day, hateful in its sameness. I am
hateful, too, cursing the everlasting sun,
the weak, idle moon. Papa doesn't know
what I am thinking. The one time Ingeborg
spoke of America, Papa's shoulders
rose, and he seemed to grow larger. He said
nothing, but his eyes touched her the way
a hammer sounds iron. Ingeborg did not
speak again, nor at the next meal, but her
words hung in the air, loud as iron's echo.

Waiting for Nothing

October 1911
Åseral, Norway

Clouds smother the mountain, the gray lake.
The river leaves the lake's far end, runs
the valley, drops to the village below,
to the church on its slabs of stone.
Passes by church, graveyard, store, road.
The road goes somewhere
I have never seen, where Ingeborg has gone.

She writes of things—ships in a harbor, water
lapping their sides like tongues. Wide docks
hewn from planks, piled high with goods
men load into ships, shouting. The slow sea.
The other side. Here there is
a farm that sits like a knot in the trunk
of a tree where a branch has broken off.

Washing Day

August 1912
Åseral, Norway

Mama calls me. Sun lights the corners,
does not reach me, tucked in bed like a hand
inside a mitten. Lake water will cool our ankles.
Bits of soap and rubbing cloth against rocks

will erase the stains of work, make thoughts
white again. The sun will reveal my hands,
their thin skin, blue veins, tiny hairs.
I will smell the watery air, watch Mama,

her head bent, her eyes only for the clothes.
Mama and I will speak few words. The sun
will stay long hours in the sky. We will
hang the clothes up near the house to dry,

their sleeves reaching in wind, their collars
remembering necks, heads, thoughts.

Aboard the *Hellig Olav*

April 1913

My back is on this bed.
The bed is on the floor.
The floor is the bottom of the ship,
a ship on the sea. I never knew
the sea was so big. The land
grew flat, fell off the edge.
I lie on this bed and wish for
a silence between waves. The wake
spreads long and wide, nine stars
a moving arrow in the sky.
The lamp swings. Shadows
wash over me like water.

In a dim shop in Kristiansand
I saw a glassblower, a hole
like the sun. In it he thrust a pipe,
drew out liquid that did not flow.
A scream caught at my throat like a hand.
The hole roared as loud as the sea.

To America

April 1913
Aboard the Hellig Olav

In the open air women's skirts whirl
around them, men's boots drum
the deck. A callused hand asks me
to dance. I pull away. They all laugh,
my cheeks flame. Ingeborg must have
danced wildly, men waiting their turns.

When I was confirmed, I quaked
at the minister's grim questions.
Ingeborg's answers flowed like water
over round stones. Sometimes my skin
is too small, and I can hardly hold within me
what I know. But I am struck dumb by a
cocky smile, my eyes blinded by other eyes.

Mama was quiet, but her stories shivered
the darkness. She told of trolls who spook
cows, make away with slow children.
Water trolls wait in the lake like logs, wait
to pull someone under. Trolls can be so big
and so old that trees sprout from their backs.
The whole forest can rise up and swallow.

I don't have Mama's stories or Ingeborg's
jabbering or the minister's stern blessings.
I am as silent as Marit lying in hard ground.
If only she could dance smoothly, smile coyly,
whisper what I could say to callused hands.

Against My Dreams

Ellis Island

April 1913

The man with the cold eye
looked in my mouth, his smooth
fingers that have never seen
work held down my tongue
with a flat bit of wood. I
might have choked, but I looked
into that cold eye and my own
coldness righted me.

The man with the warm eye
asked so many questions.
I could think only of Ingeborg
who waits for me, her chatter
filling the air like birds.
She would know what to say.
Answers would rise, dark wings
against sun. But I knew no
words, so I smiled at the man,
his warm eye, his hands knotted
from work. I kept saying
my name, the sound rising over me
like the first star in winter night:
Gunnhild Olavsdatter Breland.

And its beauty spread
like the full moon, which can
show the way even in blackness.
Breland: small pockets of snow
left in spring when sunlight
and rain wash the rest away.
That is what happened
to my name, rubbed from me,
a scrap left, an American name:
Gertrude Olsen.

Gone is the patch of snow in shadow,
Papa, Nana. A daughter is named
for her grandmother,
for her father, for the land.
The man had a warm eye, but
a cold ear, a hard, cold ear.

Once when I was a girl, growing
to woman, I walked to the church,
the miles of muddy lane leading me.
Coming back in afternoon light,
I met my own footprints, cut deep
by my tree-shoes. The late sun
cast dark lines at their edges.
As far as I could see, until
the path bent away from the river,
my steps made their way
toward me, marks on the earth,
breath in the air, a trace.
The footprints said, "You are
Gunnhild," a name that sung itself,
though I did not hear it then.

Longer Streams

May 1913
New York City

I have my own room here. I've never had my own
room before. From the mountaintop I could
look down on house and barn roofs. It's not
so different here. Below me a stone roof, and I can
imagine the slow river a lake. The trees across
the river reach like fingers through mist.

Raindrops on the window sit fast, until one swells
enough to run, and it hits another and swells
until it runs and hits another in longer
and longer streams. The river is the color
of the roof. I can put a boat inside a water bead
until it swells and drops away.

If someone asked me, I'd say the mistress has
a kind face. Her eyes shine in light like other
eyes. I don't know if my work is right. I smile
when she smiles. When I speak the words I know,
she shakes her head. She says words
I don't know, her voice steady and sharper then.

Everything here is clean and good, the bed linen,
the curtains, my uniform. The floor around the rug
is polished. The doorknobs are glass. In the mirror
the window is smaller and more dark. Once a rainbow
arched the whole valley, mountain to mountain.
It takes a long time for a boat to reach the river's end.

The Crack in the Mountain

July 1913
New York City

And what if the mountain should open, the mark
in its side parting like the Red Sea, what
would come from the mountain then?

Only owls rapped at that door without steps,
and a stream ran from under the door down
the broad mountain to join with the waters
of the deep lake. The stream's dark line
rushed to the shore and stopped.

I saw sometimes that the mountain moved,
a small ripple, like blood in Papa's neck
when he chopped at the block in sun. He
seemed not to feel it. And Mama, bent over
the flatbread griddle, did not seem to know.
The sun like a shadow on the mountain's side
kept the scar hidden sometimes, rock glazed
white as Nana's hair by the fire.

I dreamed over and over that the narrow crack
widened, and the rumble carried by wind
shook the green fields, the square stones
under the barn, the wood of the house
and my bed. Once I heard the cows moan
and the sheep scatter, their bells knocking.
I alone seemed to hear it, awake in the night's
long light. When the wind was quiet sometimes,
I could hear the mountain splitting, as steady
and slow as little Gunnvor's breathing.

If the mountain laid itself open, would it have
stomach, thoughts, blood? What would come
from the mountain then, raw and gaping? Would
it give forth its insides—snakes, bears, foxes
and elk thrown into the air like dust? Would magpies
and ravens rise like smoke from its wound?
Would the sun fly away, the lake stiffen to ice?

And what if the mountain tears itself open, what if
these great high buildings shatter, their insides spilling
with thunder worse than the stillness of snow?

Against My Dreams

November 1913
New York City

Nights I lie and build a dam
               against my dreams.
With a cruel-toothed blade
I cut trees as big as three men
and lay them one by one
across the narrows of the river.
In the cracks between
I pile rocks and stumps,
shovel upon shovel of earth.
               The water waits.

From the topmost logs a wide lake
spreads away like a vast, slick
floe of ice. Underneath,
the water gathers itself
               and waits.

It begins as a trickle
I can barely hear, but soon
the trickle joins another
               and the water spills
here, over there and there, faster
than my shovel. In sheets
it rushes over stones and mud
               and with a rumble
greater than a train
               a log is moved.
My dam scatters like straw in wind.
Now I have begun to dream
               when I'm awake.

Days I wear an apron, white
as finest porcelain, but
sometimes I forget
            to be thankful.
Nights I see Papa's face
            in the window.
He's stern, the way he used to look
in church, but always when his face
hangs there a moment, he begins to cry
            soundlessly.
And then I cry, too, and I have
no words for myself. Papa never
comes into my room. He stays
at the window, quiet
            as the moon.
The morning he drove me down
the rocky pass to the station
the sleigh whispered softly, but Papa
            had no words for me.
As I watched him drive away
toward the mountain shadows, once
he turned around and tears
sparkled on his cheeks
            like icicles.

Does Papa dream?
Once he dreamed of an angel, yes,
once an angel came to him
                    in a dream,
bigger than the biggest living man.
Papa's fever burned white hot
and even with the doctor's
bitter tonic he grew too weak
                    to open his eyes.
Then stood the angel huge and dazzling
over Papa's bed, and its slow, hollow
                    voice, more thundering
than the minister's, told him
not to take the medicine again.
Papa did as it said and then
                    the fever left him.

                    Papa dreams, or
he dreamed once. Sunday mornings
he was quietest, reading his Bible
in angled early light. Sun glowed
gold through the turning page.
When snow was too thick
for us to reach the church, Papa read
                    in the angel's voice.
Each word dropped hard like a rock
from the mountain. I wonder if
                    God looks like Papa.
But He doesn't have Papa's hands,
dry and callused. God's hands
are soft and tender like a baby's.

Papa's hands
are like his eyes. They hold on to
                what he is thinking.

                God's silence
is like the heat of a long-burning
fire, the coals lighting the darkness
                like eyes.
Sometimes I think this unspeakable hush
belongs to the Devil. And the first
glance of morning is like
                the Devil's tongue,
licking its way under my window.
                Silent as flame.
Silent as Papa's face outside,
a tiny glint of fire in his eyes.

Once when I was a small child
I stuck my hand into the fire's
last embers. Don't cry, Papa,
                please don't cry.

The Beast

January 1914
New York City

It lies between buildings, filling the streets
with the coils of its body. Its hot breath
follows me. Sometimes I can walk
unbothered, feel the smooth coldness
of air. Sometimes it slides suddenly
up from the river when I am not ready.
I have learned to be careful.

It has scales and a rearing head, and it
watches when I pick out vegetables for dinner.
Sometimes I see only the body, the head
streets away. Then it is easier
to keep to my purpose. There are days when
I round a corner and the head blocks my path.
The eyes, black and lidless, know what I think.
I cannot choose fabric or remember to stop
at the cobbler's or even know the way home.
I must wait until it lets me go.

Around the corner from the fish market
is a Roman Catholic church. I should not
go there, but I do, to see the stone woman
who stands in front. She is young
and unharmed. Her hair rings her head,
her dress hangs in even folds. She stands
squarely, arms outstretched, palms
lifted toward Heaven. Under her feet is a
long snake, its jaws straining around an apple.

Against My Dreams

Long ago chasing me through the fields, Ingeborg
looked so like a magpie I had to stop and laugh.
When I looked down, my foot was planted firmly
on an adder, just behind its rearing head.

I visit the woman on the Beast's hiding days,
look up at her smooth white face, her open palms,
the sky above. I run my finger along the snake's
body, touch the round apple of knowing.

The City

February 1914
New York City

Am I the only one who sees faces
in the clouds? A wrinkled old man
with flaring nostrils, an old woman
with burning hair. They stir and steam
and both become cows, stupid and slow,

then twisting snakes. On Sundays
the stove used to glower in church,
the Devil come to watch and crackle.
One of the men would open the door
to load some wood and tempt Him

with his hands. Here the church rises
swiftly, wanting to forget us far below.
But the light remembers. Through dazzling
windows it spreads on the floor in pools
of blood and fire, green ponds with blue

and violet fish. Sometimes I can't hear
the minister, so loud are the colors.
The city shouts outside, swallowing up
the choir. Carved monsters and angels
line the roofs and clamor at the sky.

Ships blast horns, fighting for the channel.
A fire wagon rumbles past, its wood and iron
wheels drumming the cobblestones, its bell
clanging. When I used to hear the mountain
sigh, I knew by Marit's craning neck that she

could hear it, too. When she died, I saw her
as a swan, gliding over water, her long neck
arched, eyes darting to the clouds. Or an elk,
surefooted on the mountainside, pulling at grass
with her teeth, her head snapping upright

at the crack of a branch. She could not
come to America, her body heavy with dirt.
It is a comfort sometimes when I hear
the city bawling to know that she would
hear it, too. I keep these things to myself.

The Piano

March 1914
New York City

Evenings when only the servants
are at home I sneak to the big hall,
seat myself quickly, the scrape
of the bench noisy enough to split
the ceiling. I open the long narrow door
that covers the keys, smooth as skin.
When I'm ready—it takes a long time,
the air is so loud—I sound a note.
It trembles through my finger. Then
another low one to keep the fear at bay.

And another. Sundays the organ
in the quiet church stirred the boards
under my feet, rose into the pew
and startled my ears like winter cold.
I touched its keys once when no one
was looking. Now Jon's fiddle,
Gunnvor's guitar, Papa's deep hum slide
over the cool black and white. And so
I play cascades of water, the mountain
cracked by lightning, lullabies. Rye
sweeps in a stroke of wind. Ripples flex
across the lake. Smoke curls from the fire.
Marit laughs. A sheep's bell. A star.

When stillness creeps between my notes,
one last time I touch the keys, smooth
as bone, close the narrow wooden door.
I edge my way off the long bench,
hoping no one tells the mistress.

In My Father's House

April 1914
New York City

A letter from Gunnvor, the strokes on the page
line up like fence posts:

She rose that morning and carefully dressed,
laced her good leather shoes, smoothed
the handmade petticoat over her hips,
then the dark woolen dress that Mama
sewed for this day. Even a hat, given by
old Mrs. Johannsen because Gunnvor
fed her when she could not do for herself.

Gunnvor's bags sit waiting, each closed
securely with Papa's new rope. He has
made this trip before, with Ingeborg, with me,
with Ånund, with Olav, with Gunnar,
with Jon. Each time Papa drove down
the mountain he held his face forward,
looking neither right nor left, his back straight,
not flinching, even when the wagon lurched
over gullies carved by spring rains.

He brought me in snow, the land swept
into sameness, the mountains guarding
the white road. He was as quiet as the sleigh.

I see Papa setting the bags side by side
over the runners. Mama's face is drawn
and frozen. Firmly, as if the wind might
snatch her away, Papa helps Gunnvor
to the seat, rounds the other side
and climbs in. He does not look at Mama.

With a flip of the reins, a pull, they slide away.
Gunnvor waves her handkerchief until
Mama disappears. Papa clears his throat.
Now they come to the gate, and Papa
jumps down on his heavy boots, kicks up
squalls of snow as he walks, lifts the bars
from their notches. Gunnvor sits, fidgeting.
Papa looks at the sky.

Slowly, as if there is no such thing as time,
he walks back, climbs to his seat, his breath
gathering in clouds. He looks at Gunnvor,
his face red and twisted. Like a storm
amassed that finds its first release,
he begins to cry, silently at first, and then
with his hands over his face, he sobs.

Slowly, as if there is no such thing as time,
Gunnvor takes Papa's hand, touches
his knuckles, the worn calluses on his palm.
She holds his hand, their breath rising. She nods.

Her words spill like fresh milk: "I will not go
to America, Papa. I will stay with you."

Woman of Metal

November 1914
New York City

In the small green above the river
they have set a great stone, a high table
perhaps, a place to spread a feast for giants.

One afternoon when I should have been ironing,
I traced its cold, carved letters with my finger:
Born January 6, 1411, then *May 30, 1431.*

The rest I couldn't understand, but an old woman,
gesturing from her forehead to her chest, eyes
alight with tears, read it aloud to herself:

Joan of Arc, Born St. Dominy, France,
Burned at the Stake at Rouen. She spoke it
again and again with the slowness of a hymn,

crossed herself once more and walked away,
her head bent humbly to the wind.
This morning I stopped above the river.

In the small green between streets
she had appeared, bolted to the great stone,
a metal woman atop a rushing horse.

She is dressed like a man in battle mesh,
the sword in her right hand raised to pierce
the sky. Thrust forward in the saddle,

she prods her horse with iron spurs,
the horse fierce, his mouth a cruel snarl,
his muscles hard under tooled metal trappings.

I do not know her battle, but her sword
is lifted against God. Did she burn for
fighting Him? To burn, I can't imagine it,

flames coiling at your feet like serpents,
arching up your legs to strike, swallowing you
in their wide jaws. Did you try to scream,

your voice crackling in the fire's roar, until flames
hissed your hair, your face became white light?
Or did you thank God for the burning?

Eye

May 1915
New York City

Three trolls shared an eye,
each with a hollow socket
in the middle of his forehead.
The one who had the eye
would go first, pounding
through the forest, the others
blundering behind. If the first one
grew weary or they fought about
which way to go, he would pop out
the eye and give it to the next one.
Trolls think slow thoughts
like rocks. They take what
doesn't belong to them: coins, eggs,
girls for wives, boys for supper.

On the way to confirmation lessons
cousin Ingerid and I stopped at Fjeldskleiv,
where the river tipped and dropped
to the town and church below. As
our mothers had instructed, we'd change
our carved tree-shoes for our only
leather pairs. In the middle of the river
was a troll kettle, a deep bowl in the rock
where trolls come to boil their dinner.
Ingerid and I hooked our shoes quickly,
always looking over our shoulders.

One day something came over me,
recklessness or haughtiness,
and I climbed down to the kettle, sat
on its rim, dangled my bare feet
inside. Shadows bent over the water.
Ingerid screamed, "Come away!"
I smiled, and she screamed
again, ran down the steep hill.

The river grew loud in the silence
left behind, and I sat quiet, my feet
swirled by the eddy. I sat a long time,
sound washing over my body,
shadows lengthening toward me.

Rocking in the Sky

September 1915
New York City

I wish sometimes to stop everything, to rest
from myself. When I was a child, it was enough
to rise early, awakened by Mama's stirrings.
It was enough to watch her face, to see
light spread over the floor slowly. What did I
long for then? For the cows to disappear
off the earth, or at least to give me no trouble,
no losing themselves in the forest.

When Ingeborg began her monthly bleeding,
she ran screaming, dying, to Mama and then
walked for days with a regal air. I knew to expect
my own bleeding then, for Ingeborg told me.
But I did not know it would make me quiet.

I should hope for a husband, children—
that is what women want. I float
on an ocean, stars piercing the sky.
The moon arcs like a rocking cradle.

I used to stare at clouds, stop mid-field
to hear the wind. Papa warned me of idleness,
where the Devil breeds. I go through this house
and freshen the flowers, pick off the wasting
blooms, long for things I still cannot name.

The Linen Closet

February 1916
New York City

The first time I came to this room I was struck
silent. I opened each glass door, ran my hand
down folded towels, thick as sheep's wool.
I traced embroidered letters, my rough finger
scratched the thin, glistening thread. The same
letters on sheets, pillow covers, smooth linen
napkins, white against white. I touched
every one. It took a stool to reach the top shelf
where lace tablecloths lay like snowflakes, and I
rubbed my cheek on fleece blankets, soft
as baby's hair. The room is all cedar, walls,
floor and ceiling, and the air bit at my nose
like new hay. I put my shoes by the door.

Perhaps she was eating a boiled potato—
her spoon in midair like a red eye caught
the fire's dance. Only one man in the village
had heard the sound before, but we always said
he had dreamed it. I think she rested one hand
in her lap, her thumb curled tight inside her fingers.
Her hair fell across her eyes, and she lifted a hand
to brush it aside. She was alone in the house,
thinking of Christmas, of her mother, buried
behind the church, an iron marker at her head.

"The rush of a thousand rivers," Old Thorensen
would say. Then he'd grow quiet. Perhaps

she set her doll on the bench beside her. I think
it was missing an eye. Her feet couldn't touch
the floor, she crossed and uncrossed them, heels
kicking the chair rung. The sky promised to clear.

Against My Dreams

"I heard it when I was a boy," he would say.
"The boom of a thousand felled trees, then nothing."

I come to this room every day, to sit on this stool
and hear nothing. Not the mistress' orders, the clink
of the milkman, the bell. Not even the rattle of wind.

I think that her father walked between snowdrifts,
the light held before him, his boots squawking
crows. He swung the heavy door closed, settled
the lamp on the floor. In the circle of light
he probably looked like a tree, the pitchfork
in midair a branch, his hands knotted around it.
The hay landed soft as swallows come to roost
in the eaves. Cows' breath hung in clouds.

When the silence fell from the mountain, their whole
farm vanished. Papa and the Grendessen boys
dug them out early in spring, her from the house,
him from the barn. They rolled each cow
onto boards and pulled it out tied by long ropes
to the horses. Old Thorensen died the next summer.

Every day I come to this room, to sit and hear
nothing. If I put out the lamp, I see nothing,
not even a sliver of light from under the door.

Inheritance

March 1916
New York City

Long ago in Denmark a man was spared
in the plague. He buried his family one by one,
alone and forsaken, and wandered with no purpose.
Starving, he came upon a chimney without smoke.
When he creaked the door open, he found a woman
lying in bed, cold as the fireplace. Locked
in her stiff arms was a healthy baby. He took

the boy home, fed and clothed him, taught him
his prayers, taught him to work until the last
light of day. But the child grew prideful, disobedient,
loud. One day he threw a stone at his stepfather's
prize goose. The man chased the boy
with a stick, his face flaming, his eyes iced

with rage. The child ran, found his way to a wharf,
stowed on a ship in a corn bin. He landed
at Bergen in Norway, and his uncle, a big man
with a soft voice, took him in, taught him
to be a tailor. The boy learned how to make
tiny stitches and hidden knots, how to be frugal
with cloth. He grew to manhood, inherited the shop,

and prospered. One day robbers ambushed
the King's men, stole coins meant for the King,
escaped to the north. The tailor and his friend
went after them, came to a place where a woman
sat weeping, her dress torn. When they asked
if she had seen the robbers, she pointed to her barn,
whispered that it had been terrible. The three

Against My Dreams

made a plan. With the two men crouched behind,
the woman walked to the barn, swished her skirts
and clucked as if feeding her hens. The tailor
leapt out at the robbers, wrestled their guns away
and shot them. Then he said he should have all
the gold, for he had been so brave. His friend said
they should split it in half. The tailor killed his friend
with a robber's gun and fled, the bags of money

heavy on his back. He came to our valley, courted
a woman whose parents said she couldn't marry him
because he had an evil look. He bought farm
after farm until he could walk on his own land
from the mountain all the way to where the church
now stands. Then her parents decided that she
would be happy, so there was a splendid wedding

with many horses. The bride and groom made
Breland their home, the logs of our walls hewn
by his hands, the great kettle over our fire stirred
by hers. They lived to see their children's
children's children. One of their descendants

was Papa. It is told that the tailor hid the rest
of the treasure in a coffeepot, buried in the hills.
Many people dug for it. Papa laughed at the story,
but I saw him wandering, a shovel in his hand.

Dark Petal

May 1916
New York City

Sometimes I brush my hair far more
than I have to, to feel the softness
of the bristles streak down its long length.

Gathered to one side, my hair is a black iris.
It spreads over my shoulder, opens at my breast.
I brush it more, the shine glowing in lamplight, darkly.

Each morning I pull it tight against my head,
roll it, roll it, twist it into the bun I build at my neck.
No one knows then of the dark petal, the sleek

undone length of it, a secret I let down in the evening,
the secret I take to bed in two long braids, woven
of shine, that twist about me in the night.

Sunday Afternoon

July 1916
New York City

The sun was hot in the sky.
My back still feels its heat, my arm

the slight ghost of his hand.
Songs of birds fluttered

in the leaves, drifting to the ground
around us as we walked. His voice

washed the flat earth, replenished
its dryness. My words fell like pebbles.

I tripped over them piled at my feet.
He did not seem to notice, turned

his smile toward me. He says
I am beautiful, my dark hair,

wide cheekbones, blue eyes.
No one has said such a thing

before. His pale hair is a crown.
I dared hold his hand.

Wedding Night

April 1917
New York City

Ingeborg laughed at me
when I asked her.

Andrew's eyes
shimmer in lamplight.
And he dances
like satin. He says
I am beautiful.

Mama would say,
"You are a woman now,
taking your rightful place
in God's plan."
Mama would wrap me
in her strong arms, rock me
slowly
until I believed her.

The Yule Chair

April 1917
New York City

In the old days
they set out great carved bowls
for Christmas Eve:
one with water,
one with milk,
one with ale,
one with brandy.

They took their best clothes,
hung them over the chairs,
and walked around the table
three times.

They sat down in the chairs
and went to sleep, their heads
nestled in their arms.
The unmarried ones dreamed.

The one who came first
into the dream you would marry.
If this man or this woman
drank of the brandy,
you would be rich.
If it was the ale,
you would be lucky.
If it was the milk,
you would be unlucky.
If it was the water,
you would be
very poor.

This is the way
Mama first saw Papa.
She never told us
from which bowl
he drank.

PART II: 1917~1939

Wedding Day, 1917

Gunnhild and her husband, Andrew Stensen

Gunnhild's Son

Arthur Norman Stensen,
born in 1918

Gunnhild's Daughter

Thelma Stensen,
born in 1919

As a girl Thelma longed for
a middle name, but her father
told her that "Thelma" was too
beautiful to be sullied by another
name.

With Child

December 1917
New York City

Ingeborg carries her baby on her hip as if
it fell from the sky and she caught it squarely.
I am not like Ingeborg.
What will I do with a small crying thing?

I wish for Mama. She had a gift
for birthing—women miles away sent for her.
She knew what to do when a baby wasn't
right, born foot first, walking before thought.

I try to think good thoughts so I'll have
a baby with good bones.
But before I know it, fear rises like a sigh,
sits in my throat. Cuckoos lay their eggs
in magpie nests, let magpies hatch them.

Yesterday I spilled a glass of milk, cold
whiteness spreading over the table, streaming
to the floor. I had to sit down, stare at the spot
where wall and ceiling touch, a straight line.

Unclean Touch

Everything I touch is smeared
                      with something,
mud or grease or excrement. I hide them,
sheets, skirts, undergarments, but the filth
                      only grows
until it reaches the sight of others. They pretend
not to notice. I try to wash my dress but only
ruin it, spread the blotches wider and wider
                      for all to see.
At the dreaming's end I bear a dirty baby, the blood
of birth dark on its face, its cry pitiful. I swathe it
in grimy rags, kiss the stained cheeks. The cries
are quieted, a smile quivers over the lips. Then
                      it lies cold in my arms.

Arthur Norman Stensen

January 1918
New York City

He is round and soft and needs everything.
He sucks at my breast and then sleeps.
He's a rock thrown into the water.
I wash him, feed and clothe him,
hold him when he cries out.
He is sand moved by the river.

I tell him what I'm thinking.
I tell him when the air looks dark,
though sunlight fills the corners of the room.
When he cries, I tell him stories of maidens
carried off by trolls and forced to marry them.
I speak of the sounds I hear at night,
the scraping of wind on glass,
the spilling of moonlight all over the floor.
And he listens.

Demons

July 1921
New York City

The days go better when I don't think, when
one task comes after another like feet walking.

Dusting moves morning to noon, dishes bring
evening in a slow, measured way. Watchful,
I have to keep fluttering thoughts quiet, or
suddenly the floor is not flat, the furniture is not

where I left it. Rooms become the future and past
I live in, foggy and strange like the morning river.
Sometimes I see Mama in the mirror. She doesn't
look beyond the hot iron's weight, where thoughts

can singe cloth and flesh. My thoughts
face each other over a deep channel, thrust
their muscled arms across and pull. Weaker ones
fall in, then more take their places, pull and push,

and the channel boils with their bodies.
Ingeborg is content with a man and two children,
laughs easily, loves to dance. Grime smears
her windowsills. But people were made for work,

cast out of the Garden by haughtiness. Papa
used to say there are two kinds of people,
the lazy and the good. Heaven is for the good.
I look in the mirror and smile, but my face

could crack. It was molded for duty
like the Queen's china cup. There are times
when I stand by my sleeping children, feel warm
as summer rain. Leaves dip one at a time, touched

Against My Dreams

by single drops. There are times when Andrew,
so full of ideas, spreads blueprints on the table
after dinner, in the air traces buildings I can see.
He took me to 54th Street where a building higher

than any church steeple rose out of his head.
Even Papa would sit back on long summer nights,
nod to Jon's fiddle, Gunnvor's guitar. Lines in his face
grew softer then. Ingeborg says I think too much.

The Firecrests

February 1925
New York City

Faces in the street are full of eyes,
too many things are pulling at me.
Thelma can hardly breathe, pneumonia

filling her lungs. Her birth was so easy
I hardly remember it. Now she lies
in a hospital room. Only her eyes

move, barely move, staring at ships
that ease out to sea. I made her go
to school, told her it was only a cold.

The doctors had to make a hole
between her ribs to drain the choking fluid.
They say she will not live.

Each day I sit beside her bed and match
my breaths to hers. Each morning
Arthur cries. He doesn't understand

why she disappeared. Marit haunts me
in the night, keeps me from sleep, her eyes
wide, her cheeks blazing. She says

nothing, mixes her breaths with mine.
Andrew seems to think he can make me
laugh. When he walks down the front stairs

on his hands and bounces grinning to his feet,
I cry. But it works for Artie, who tumbles
down the steps, lands in a heap, and giggles.

Evenings Andrew holds Thelma's hand,
plays with her hair, returns her thin smile
with a funny face. I think he is at the bottle,

but his sorrow is so big it could explode
into a thousand pieces, each spinning
endlessly in a thousand directions.

Once I stood in the upper field and a raven
flapped overhead, chased by a dozen tiny
firecrests. They rose and dove, bombarding

the raven as it fled squawking toward the woods.
They pursued, as if attached by strings. It paused
on a high branch, and they swarmed like bees.

The raven could do nothing to escape. It flew
from tree to tree, its tormentors fastened by
their tough strings, following, always following.

The House

September 1926
New York City

There must be a way to fit together,
your light hair with my dark, your
round blue eyes with mine.
There must be a way to speak of this.

I dreamed of a house you built, where
everything had its proper place.
Sofas matched draperies, windows
viewed a garden sculpted carefully
by hands. Each room led to the next
in perfect order. There was cleanness
and quiet and light. Perhaps there is
some way I can fit myself to you.

When we sleep, the lines of my legs
trace the lines of your legs, my back
against your stomach and chest.
I breathe with your breath, the cadence
of our hearts one cadence.

I listen to your voice and remember
why we married, the way my eyes
looked into yours without half-closed
or trembling lids. Your hand reached
for mine at the table where we took
our meals, its smoothness warm
against my cool, rough fingers.

Against My Dreams

In this house I dreamed of, everything
had its function: a window seat
above the apple tree, a lamp to sew by
at the deepest chair. No interrupted lines,
nothing in the way of the view. I walked
through the house slowly, trying to
understand its order, almost at home.
I came upon you, intent over a broad table
in bright light, blueprints spread before you,
your pencil writing calculations.

New Dress

October 1929
New York City

Yesterday morning I sat at the kitchen table,
feet braced against the floor. If someone
asked me was it night or day, I wouldn't know
the answer. Or the name of the day, or the year.
Or the country. The way I used to be, following
cows, sitting in the woods with my sewing. Needle
rarely met the limp cloth draped over my knees.

Then the snap of a twig, the startled jump. I'd force
myself to face the sound, sit with all those eyes
between trees, shadows spreading over my skin.

Yesterday morning at the table, my hands folded
in my lap—a dry twig snapped. I willed myself
to turn toward the sound, the little blonde head.
I saw the flush of her skin, heard some words:
birthday party . . . dress too small . . . Mother?

This morning I pushed my right foot, my left foot,
across the floor, down the stairs to the street. I took
the money I'd saved since last year, for my coat,
and the egg money. I saw it in a window—a dress
blue as her eyes, its ribbon belt crowned by a rose.

She came home from school to the waiting box,
touched the long edge before she lifted the cover,
and as if it were alive, set it tenderly on the bed.
She opened the rustling paper, saw the pale lace,
her eyes big, then hugged the dress against her.
"Oh, Mother, thank you, thank you," whirling.

It was still daylight when I peeled potatoes, cut cool
whiteness into chunks, filled the pot with clean water.

Against My Dreams

Visitors

April 1930
New York City

Nights I lie next to Andrew, his body
a weight that pushes the bed down, sinks
me. Things visit in the darkness.
I could name them, but those would not be
their real names. They don't speak.
They leave only when they're ready.

Sometimes I doze into dreams—
Ingerid shows off her new hat, Gunnvor
perches on the hill imagining a husband,
Mama spins soft wool into yarn,
Papa plows, the horse's muscles taut.
They all flicker like sunlight among leaves.

This morning there was a new dream—
I could not get ready. My dress
needed ironing. One shoe was missing.
When I opened the painted chest
to take out the wedding things, I found
moth holes in the tightly woven rug,
a mouse nest in the embroidered linen.
I had no traveling bag. I took care of
one thing, mending the rug, but
something else fell apart in my hands.

When I awoke, the sun betrayed
streaks on the windows. If
I were to stay, I would wash them, sitting
on the sill to reach the outer panes
with my rag, hanging over the street below.
I need not to smell Andrew's breath.
The children need to count on supper.

The dark ones sit heavy on the bed, watching.
I could be glad for their company.
Bending over the washboard, scrubbing a stain
from the sheet, I would know I'm not alone.
Mama and Papa vanish in morning light.

Cracks in the Sidewalk

October 1930
New York City

Women with gardens growing from their hats,
men in black bowlers: I walk among them
in my simple dress, cross the street
in my only pair of shoes. Do they notice
those cracks in the sidewalk
where weeds manage to flower?

Andrew is flat like the portrait on the parlor wall,
gone to Florida where there is still plenty, enough
to build big hotels. He sends money back.
It doesn't erase the image of the bottle in his hand.
Safe at my brothers' farm, the children eat
three meals a day, run wild through tall grass.
I can't keep them there forever. I work
when I can find it. The rich never want
to touch their own dirt. But it gets harder
and harder. Too many people have less
and less. I write to Mama and lie.

I can no longer picture Andrew, his crooked smile,
his sky blue eyes, on Sundays so handsome
in his fine white collar. Now he's as flimsy
as paper. I'd like to put a match to him.

My Small Heart

May 1931
New York City

My chest is stone, huge as the domed hall
of Ellis Island. And in it flutters a tiny heart.
I only guess that it beats, for I cannot feel it.
I can feel only the vast hard vault.

I dreamed Andrew fell at my feet. I kneeled,
opened his mouth, breathed into him life.
He woke, startled, his eyelids like leaves
in a storm. Then I dreamed he took his own life—
how, I don't know. I remember only the flood
of people come to comfort me. I was suddenly
a child; I shrank from them, running, screaming,
my arms flailing, my wits scattered like chaff.

Andrew is dead. Over and over my mind
tells me. But my heart trembles in its vault
and says it can't be so. What can I believe?
A wooden box lowered by straps into a hole,
a few words, a few shovels of dirt? His eyes
were flat circles of sun behind fog. Fever,
coughing, blood at the corner of his mouth.

Against My Dreams

But he died long before that. He'd hide
bottles in the water closet, shut himself up
in the bedroom for days. I begged Thelma
to pour the brown stuff down the sink—
he'd never blame her. Sometimes
when I heard his loud songs coming home,
I hid with Thelma under the stairs. "Why
are we hiding, Mother?" she'd ask, but
I made no answer because I didn't know.
I heard her tell a playmate once that his
crooked walk was from his sailor days.
Artie was often silent, but then he'd
slam the door, a whip-crack, and flee.

Diamond stickpin in his lapel, his eyes
blue suns, Andrew took me for his wife.
His voice sang the words like a hymn.
The same suit wrapped that bundle of sticks
inside the coffin, diamond long gone. Words,
a few shovels of dirt, the cover a shut door.

Crow

August 1931
North Canton, Connecticut

Papa hates crows. He'd always curse
their flapping over the rye, their perching
on the barn roof. "Rotten," he'd say.
"Nothing good can come of them."
This crow squawks enough to make me
listen. It wants to tell me something.

The light among leaf shadows
glimmers like water. I sit here
and shuck peas in my brothers' garden.
Andrew is dead. I'll never get used to it.

Thelma asks each morning how I know
it's really true. She said she went
behind the church to the cemetery, pretended
a grave for him there, a marble stone etched
with the golden letters, "Father," the corners
carved into angels that sit on his shoulders.

To her he is an angel still, and I'm the Devil's
friend. She demands to know why I left him
alone to drink, protects him so fiercely
that she has no tears. Artie doesn't say much.

The crow has flown off. A twig fallen
from an oak snaps at a touch, so supple
on the tree. When Marit died, I thought about
bones cracking under the weight of earth.

Being right lets me live from dawn to dark,
dark to dawn, week after week. Love snapped
like a twig every time Andrew hid a bottle
in the umbrella stand, out on the fire escape.

I was right to leave him, to send the children
away, to work until I couldn't sleep from tiredness.
Peas fill the deep pot, pods at my feet like leaves.

A crow flies over the field. A flock of smaller birds
screeches after it. They swoop and rise, driving
the crow farther off. The black specks fade.

Cross

October 1931
New York City

Cut stones cost money.
Artie made
a wooden cross,
carved deep
with a knife
little crooked letters:
Andrew Stensen.
Born 1893.
Died 1931.
They wouldn't let us
put it up at the cemetery.

No More

November 1931
New York City

I can't make bread out of stones.
Thelma's coat is too small.
Artie has no shoes.
We have just three more potatoes.
She can hardly bend her arms
or button it though she has grown thin.
One sole finally cracked completely.
Cardboard will last only so long.
The rich must be polishing their own
silver, cooking their own roasts.
The other sole flaps like a tongue, held
for a while by layers of string he wrapped
carefully around it, but then his toes erupted.
Finally I found Andrew's old pair, still
in the closet. Artie has to stuff
them with newspaper, but at least
he can walk on cold pavement.
She tried Andrew's overcoat, her arms
swallowed in sleeves, the hem
dragging the floor. I cut it into pieces.
Nights I sew the wool to fit
her slight shoulders. For now
she wears my coat to school.
I wear sweaters to look for work, to stare
at meat in the market. There is nothing
more to pull from the closet, no bread
from the oven, no milk. Soon
no roof or walls. We must go to my brothers
again, to the hiss of milk in the pail,
the snap of the wood fire.
More mouths for them to feed.
Here we will be eaten up, nothing but crumbs.

Land of Milk and Honey

June 1932
North Canton, Connecticut

The cow is big-bellied and sturdy. She stands solidly
on four hooves, her tail swishing. I pull the pink teats
one by one by one, and the warm white milk shoots
straight into the pail. Here the sun rises over green
trees and sets over green trees. Seedlings split

the earth. I can watch them grow if I sit silent, hands
folded in my lap. The children grow, too, running
long-legged over open fields, lovely stems about to
flower. My brother Gunnar is jolly, his round face red
from sun. Olav is the quiet one, his rough hands doing

his talking with a hoe. They can use a woman here.
Nights are short and hushed, dreams welcome for once,
and I can feel my blood stirred by the breaking sun.
The cock crows early, the cows wait musky and full
for my hands. It's easy to rise, dress quickly, wrap

my long hair into its bun. I'm often the first awake,
queen of this land. If only Mama and Papa could be
here, their heads nodding together. The pail
brims, I pour the whiteness into a tall can. Later
I'll skim the risen cream. We will have butter.

Now I'll go among the chickens to search for eggs,
then crack them into the big iron skillet over flame.
Sunlight will slant through the kitchen window, its rays
guiding my hands. One will hold the loaf, the other
work the knife's clean blade—my morning prayer.

Against My Dreams

New Job

November 1932
North Canton, Connecticut

I must send you away.
                        The big house
            where I will work has room for me,
                                    none
for you. I am lucky to find it.
            Mahogany tables to dust,
                              oak floors to wax,
                      someone else's
lace-trimmed sheets.

There were times when I told you
to pour the bottle down the drain.
                              Your father
            would never get angry at you.
            Life stings.
            For your sake I must not feel too much.
Your brother is like your father was.
            He thrashes around
                  to keep from drowning
                                    and sinks.
            So many days he doesn't speak.

Both of you will board with strangers,
                        you with an old couple, he
            with the family next to the parsonage.
                                    Without me
            it's too hard for my brothers
                        to keep children.
You receive the news with a cool eye,
            his eyes grow wide. You say
                                    nothing.

      Leaving,
      arriving among strangers.
                  It's good you know that early.

Watching Over Artie

April 1933
New York City

Why do I think of it now—that day
six years ago when Thelma came home from school
to find bloody rags and Artie on the kitchen table,
the doctor's hands and knife down his throat.
She screamed, "Don't kill my brother," lunged
to hit the doctor, but I grabbed her arm, pushed her
from the room. "It's just his tonsils," I tried to tell her.
"The doctor isn't killing him." Then the doctor said,
"He's bleeding more than I want him to," and I
had to go for more water and more rags.

All night she kept sneaking into Artie's room to watch
his chest move up and down. The next morning
when he finally woke, she poked him in the eye
in her mad rush to be close to him. All day
whatever he asked she would do. She hung
out the window and shouted down to the big boys
that he had a new aggie. She fed him ice cream
with his old baby spoon and never took a bite herself.
All day she barely spoke to me, sent me stern
old woman looks as if I'd been the one with the knife.

One Thing Turning

May 1934
New York City

Papa does not see this sky, this sun,
the clouds that glide over it.
He no longer tilts his head back,
his eyes rising to God in the glare.
The letter in my hand says this.

I try to imagine the box, dirt thrown
against dull wood. I try to imagine
his grave next to Marit's small one,
behind the church under bare trees.

Once I found an iron marker,
propped against the church wall.
I could make out only a few letters,
one number, the rest eaten away.
I touched it and chunks of rust
broke off. Papa said old graves have
no use, are given to the newly dead.

I want to stop this, one thing turning
into another, bones to soil, trees to smoke.

No. Papa walks upon this earth,
his wooden shoes thudding against rocks.
He hammers hot metal, pitches hay,
stands in a blaze of morning light,
his shadow reaching all the way to the lake.

Words

October 1934
New York City

Papa can't hear the wind at night. I imagine
a grave with a stone cross, a grave too small
for him. I would lay flowers at his head,
the orchids I've seen here in windows,
pile them higher and higher, keep piling them.
I imagine Mama and Gunnvor sitting tall
in their wooden pew, reaching for the minister's
words. Papa never saw my children.

I dreamed of him, alive, shouting. The elders
of the church silenced him with their sharp blades,
cut out his tongue. Words rose in my throat,
softly at first, more like noises, without my
willing them. My voice grew louder, my words
his words. I shouted what they would not hear,
shouted until the church walls rattled.

If I could see him one last time, my words
would be so small they wouldn't find my voice.
But I would look at him, his carved face,
his wild white hair. I would not look away.

Against My Dreams

The True Mother

January 1935
New York City

When two women stood before King Solomon,
both claiming the same baby, the king decreed
that the boy be cut in two, so each woman
could have half. One woman cried out,
"Oh, my lord, give her the child, don't kill him."
The second cried that if she couldn't have
the boy, then neither should have him—
she urged the swordsman on.

Thelma writes that she needs a winter hat.
I send her sanitary napkins each month
because she's ashamed to buy them herself.
Artie writes that he will get a job stoking fires
at the axe factory before and after school.
I send money for their room and board,
whatever spare coins I can.

Thelma is a good girl, obedient and quiet,
does well in school. Artie has an angry streak
but a soft spot for his sister, will give her half
his apple when she doesn't even ask.
They don't complain. If only we could have
a house that smells like warm bread and pie.

God spoke through King Solomon, who
commanded that the living child be given to
the true mother. I wish King Solomon could
tell me why God would slice a mother in half.

Moving the House

September 1938
New York City

I don't know how to think of the house anymore.
Out the tiny window upstairs the lake drew a shape
I remember. I don't know what to see out there
now, how tree shadows angle the shore,
whether sun glints from the schoolhouse window.

After Papa died, Ånund and Jon went back
to help Mama with the farm. The government said
all the land belonging to one farm had to lie together,
so Mama and Ingerid's father traded fields. Now
our farm follows one side of the lake, unbroken.

Ånund and Jon had to take apart the house and barn,
stone by stone, log by log, board by board, rebuild them
on a spot in the new field. They numbered the pieces,
moved them by wagon, day after day, put the puzzle
back together. This is what children do for their mother.

Against My Dreams

I Thought God Had Heard Me

November 1939
Hartford Hospital, Hartford, Connecticut

Maybe it was fighting those three Swedes
behind the tavern when Artie tried to prove
Norwegians are better—they left him for dead.
Or his old convertible missing the curve,
his body flying headlong into that tree.

I thought God had finally heard me
when Artie graduated, when he and Thelma
found a few rooms to rent together. Artie saved
enough money to send her to Mount Vernon
for her senior class trip. In the picture she laughs,
blonde hair shining, her classmates around her.

Thelma says it started with small things,
his socks, the time for dinner, buttoning his shirt.
But it grew and grew until Artie forgot
how to get to work, couldn't find home.

Thelma says she doesn't know why.
The doctor offers a word: schizophrenia.

I boarded the bus to Connecticut, the road
straight and narrow. I climbed wide stairs
to the hospital, walked quiet halls to his room.
He doesn't remember who I am.

PART III: 1941~1980

Gunnhild's Parents

Else Olavsdatter Eikil (1856-1946)
and Olav Ånundsson Breland (1847-1934)

The Long Waiting

December 1941
New York City

I look beyond the dust, small bits of light
whirling through the wide streets, and see
the river. And then the hills of trees.
Beyond the hills, only more dust that bites

the throat. A long time since words
came from Norway, soldiers raising dust
on roads where I walked. I load a box
with cans of meat, with wool sweaters

and don't know if it arrives, a sound
I send into cold air. No echo returns
from the mountainside. I have heard
of people eating the bark of trees, pounded

into flour, kneaded into bread. Of men
imprisoned for hiding radios in barn eaves
and stove bellies. Of coastal men
made to search for mines in icy boats

that know only fishing. I have heard so little.
Mama, Gunnvor, her children and husband,
do they sleep with their eyes open, tiptoe
through long afternoons when airplanes singe

the mountaintops? Here I work each day, and
every napkin I fold, every slick floor I mop
forces my arms down, forces my voice
to a tiny whisper. I would scramble

down the stairs, slam the door behind,
scream into the dust. I would run
over the river to the hills beyond, my arms
like spinning windmills. But I bring my hands

to my task, my stiff fingers one by one.
I talk them into polishing the silver, rubbing
thick paste over dullness, rubbing
steel gray into shine. Artie is safe at least.

He lives in his bathrobe now, his slippered feet
wandering halls of blank faces. Thelma says
he does not smile, his eyes murky. For once
I can be thankful for his sadness, his forgetting,

his wild fluttering words. They keep him from
a uniform and boots, his hands soft and white,
his feet muted against hard floors. They say men
go to war, women wait. But Mama and Gunnvor

are fighting something: dark mornings,
meager afternoon light, snow piled
halfway up the windows. The air crashing
with silence. Night after endless iron night.

Against My Dreams

Missing

January 1945
New York City

I have had a letter. Mama and Gunnvor live.
Mama's eyes must be clouded now, her hair
white as stars. I wonder if Gunnvor has
these wrinkles at the corners of her eyes.

It is Thelma now who waits for letters. Walter
has vanished in the snow, his soldier's boots
etched with water marks. Does he walk and eat
and breathe, a cigarette jaunty in his mouth,
or did his blood turn the snow red, his veins
grow dry and hard? She has had a telegram.

Thelma is swollen with a child. To make room
for her belly she ties button to buttonhole
at the top of her skirt. She had to sell the car, climbs
the hill to the bus stop for the long ride to work.
If it's a boy, she'll call it David, the little one
who fights. I send her money when I can.
She writes polite notes back, asks after my health.

I never wanted her to marry him.
She was the fine line between light and dark,
so like her father she can tell all his stories, sing
his songs. On her wedding day I made her cry—
how could she leave me behind?

I never wanted her to marry him, and now
he's nowhere, a whole regiment gone.

If Walter is found, I'll say a prayer of thanksgiving
to the hard God who rules us. His mercy is frugal,
His anger beautiful, His forgiveness harsh.

The Train

April 1945
New York City

Why did I dream of him—Andrew—
his clean blue eyes? There we were—
on a crowded train, his face next to mine.
I could see the moving windows in his eye.

I would have touched him, but he laughed
with all those people on holiday, shared
their bread, their cigars, spoke to everyone
but me, in his city clothes, with his city airs.

My bones lie heavy, carving channels
in the mattress. I thought life was more
than this: thick draperies opened in mornings,
closed nights. Bones that don't want to stand.

There should be light through colored glass,
shimmering the floor with red and gold
and green, shadows of bare branches
streaked against orange and blue.

On the platform, the train edging away,
I stared at the windows, at myself looking back.

Against My Dreams

Thanksgiving

August 1945
New York City

For Walter, who came home
skinny and limping,
his hair gone, his teeth
loose and black, and
for David, born so early
and yellow he had to live
for two months in a glass box,
I thank You
because I promised.

Mama's Voice

December 1946
New York City

Sometimes when we did our washing
at the lake, scrubbed collars against rocks,
spread linens to whiten in sun, Mama
would talk. Eikil by the River, where
she grew, was haunted by trolls
and *hulder*, and she herded the cows
with an eye over her shoulder.
When she came to Breland as a bride,
it was God's voice that spoke to her.
With each child she bore, the footsteps
of troll and *hulder* sounded farther off,
their grunting and chanting harder to hear.

One day when we sat among drying clothes,
Mama shivered, leaned into the wind.
She told of *hulder*, those lovely women
who came out of woods and fields to join in
village celebrations. Their voices were
as soft and golden as their unbraided hair.

They waited until midnight to come
when the ale bowl was empty—
and their strangeness would go unnoticed.
They danced, faster, faster, their skirts full,
their bare feet blurring. Only the watchful
would see under the skirt's widest swing
the tail that hung like a long cow's tail.
A sleepy child or lovestruck man could
vanish, unknowing or knowing too late.

Against My Dreams

It almost happened to Mama as a girl.
Tante screamed in time when she
spied the tip of that tail brush the floor,
and Mama fled to Nana's warm skirts.
It was longing I heard in Mama's voice.

I hold this letter from Gunnvor in my hand.
Mama's grave must be a lie. I can still hear
the laugh she saved for washing day. She
even took down her hair, let wind lift it
toward sun. In moonlight or when daylight
comes at a certain angle through the trees
on my soapy hands, I can still almost feel
a tail swinging from the end of my spine.

Holding Mama

August 1947
New York City

I dreamed of Mama,
    lifted her in my arms, held her
        close,
           her head
      warm on my chest.
She weighed hardly anything.
      I rocked her slowly, gently.
    Her white hair
    smelled like a baby's, sour
           and sweet.

    I close my eyes
        and see
  Breland under the mountain.
      The lake is calm,
    tall grasses buzz
        with summer.
Mama stands in the kitchen
    roasting coffee beans
      in the big black pan.
Her face is full and soft,
    her hands sure.

Against My Dreams

Stranger

October 1948
New York City

Papa had a chair, made by his grandfather,
a section of a great log slabbed off for a seat,
the curved back left covered with bark.
Around the edge of the seat was a perfect
row of teeth. Mama said in old times people
pounded into the wood their children's lost
teeth, so the chair would get the toothaches
meant for them. Papa believed it enough
that some of our teeth finished the row.

I wish I could put all my strangeness into a chair.
I'd gather up my hair and bones and teeth,
weave them tightly into a sturdy seat, carve them
carefully into a strong back. I wish I had a chair
to hammer myself into, to complete the circle.

If I Had My Own Kitchen Table

December 1948
New York City

It would be spotless, napkins laid crisp
and straight, polished silver lined up
beside fine china plates with filigree edges.

I'd serve platters of steaming beef and swordfish,
smooth gravy, Christmas-cabbage from the garden,
potatoes whipped glossy. There would be

a basket heaped with braided rolls, pats of butter
shaped like roses. My hair would glow in light
from tapers in their matching candlesticks. I'd

offer grace without halting words. My hands
that passed the food would be soft, my nails
unbroken. For dessert: strong coffee, rich

princess-cake, *krumkaker*, almond *kringle*. I'd
smile and nod at every face around the table,
glad for family. I'd never want the meal to end.

Against My Dreams

New Citizens

March 1949
Cromwell, Connecticut

On the way to the granite courthouse
Walter chatted—when might the baby come.
I looked at my hands, roughened
by soap and scrubbing, veins rising blue
under the flush of work. I curled one hand
into a fist, squeezed, the bones strong inside.
Out the car window the new world flashed by,
trees on the hillsides blushing with buds.

Among gray metal desks a woman younger
than Thelma went over my forms, read out
my answers: Norway. New York City. Housework.
Two children. Husband dead. Housework.
I nodded and nodded. I raised my hand, repeated
solemn words. I am a citizen of the United States.

At their apartment a note from Thelma: gone
with a neighbor to the hospital. So we sped there
in the long green car, a seed ready to burst.
Two hours later Linda was born. Tonight I stood
a long time at the nursery window, watched
her tiny hands curling into fists, uncurling, her skin
transparent as fine porcelain and brand new.

Laundry Day

April 1949
Cromwell, Connecticut

The clothes on the line move of their own will.
The dresses turn their backs to me. I've heard them
gossip with the neighbors in their strange tongue.

When I take them down, pin by pin, the shirts
point their long fingers. They know what I'm thinking.
The basket grows heavy with them.

Inside, where the windows are bright and strong,
I iron them into obedience. The hot metal scorches
their intentions. In the closets they keep quiet.

Marked

February 1951
New York City

How did it come, this thumbprint of God
on my forehead? Softly at first, I think,
like a smudge of dust.
                    It darkened so
slowly that no one could see it coming,
not even me. When I talk to someone, it
is what speaks, at church, in a shop, even
at the dinner table. Some relative of Cain,
                    I am marked.
Perhaps it comes from the inside,
through brain and skull and flesh.
I imagine rubbing the skin raw
with a rough cloth, the bite of bleach
in my nostrils, but I have never tried
                    to take it off.
Chosen by God or the Devil,
                    touched,
                    taken up, no longer
merely my own. At night it's invisible,
but I can feel it then, solid as coal. I
hardly dare move, lie awake on my back,
the mark above my eyes smoldering. I
hardly dare think, afraid it will spark
into flame, spread over my face, my body,
and I'll roar through the world
                    burning everything.

Green Evening

June 1952
Cromwell, Connecticut

Small Linda runs on her short legs. She
squeals, falls, rights herself. Somewhere
in me is she who rights herself. The one

who stands, sits tall, knows even when she
doesn't know. I could let my mind wander
among green stars, sleep a green sleep.

Linda holds out her hands, beckons me.
She tugs me about her yard, her round hand
in my rough one, her steps quick against

my bigger strides. We touch pine needles,
lined bark, listen to the trickling of birds. I like
to walk, one foot solid before the other.

I like to scan the lush grass. Sometimes
my eyes are so sharp. Without even bending,
the waning sun on my back, I can see every

single blade of grass. Thelma and Walter
marvel at this, David and Linda can hardly
believe it: from my full height to reach

down into cool grass, my hand sure on the
four-leaf clover, to pinch its slender stem,
rise, and hold it cupped in my hand.

Against My Dreams

Eulogy for Ingeborg

August 1953
New York City

She called me "Queenie" behind my back.
She hops in the shadows, a magpie

hunting fat mice, perches on a low branch
chattering others away from sweet

plums. She is the one who goes first—
to America, marriage, childbirth. She stashed

dirty dishes in the parlor stove, hid her beer
in the well, cursed, kept no secrets, told

a good joke. She is a window, neither inside
nor outside, clear. The one who tests the water.

She swings on a birch treetop, the whole sky
spread out above her, the wind flying by.

Morning Fire

January 1954
New York City

       My hair is on fire.
It begins each day, slowly, in the morning
as I brush, the ends of my hair warm against
my back. It creeps slowly up the length of it,
a heat at first and then bits of flame,
and I always think I can smother them,
                batting at my head
with the flat of my hand, palms pressed
against my scalp to keep out the air. But
as soon as one flame is extinguished,
the singe smell rising around me, another
flame ignites and soon another, and my hands
                are too tired and too few.
I sit then before the mirror and watch the spikes
of fire burst around my head. My hair never
burns completely—always enough is left
for the following day, to smolder, to erupt
                in dim morning light.
It is flame without heat, merely to be watched,
almost cool. I gather it up, hair and fire,
and twist it carefully into a bun, as spears
of flame keep flashing all around my head.
                But there is no controlling it.
The light catches in my eyes, where the flames
flare again one by one into blazing. A hundred
small fires in my eyes as I stare at myself
burning, cold and smokeless. Morning after
                morning I watch myself burn.

                                          Against My Dreams

Ingeborg's Sister-in-Law

July 1955
North Canton, Connecticut

Ragne feeds her garden and has enough
vegetables for winter. In her sitting room
the clock ticks, the only sound.
What would I see if I looked through her skin
to her bones behind the doctor's fluoroscope?

Each morning a soft voice, a ready hand
to make the coffee. She spends her days
cleaning, canning, weeding, milking,
each day the same, changing only
as the seasons change. The clock ticks
and she does not desire or question.

Ragne is my sister now, Ingeborg dead
these two years. Ingeborg, too, woke
to light, slid her hand past knotty days.

Morning pokes me, reminds me I have never
really settled. Crossing an ocean does not mean
arriving. The new land waits, the old land waits.

To sit under a tree, to watch the splash of light
upon grass—just for this one day, let it be enough.

The Face

September 1956
Cromwell, Connecticut

Someone stands silent, hiding
in that room.
I must pass it all day,
back and forth,
that darkened room,
its furniture sitting
like stumps.
I slip past
the doorway,
not breathing,
the air like chair stuffing.
I want to run
to the attic where
there are no curtains,
and my bed is bathed in light.
I would have to go through
that room
to get to the stairs.
If I looked,
sun like a knife
would slit between the draperies,
and I would see the face.

Thelma doesn't know.
When she and Walter come home
from work, when the children
come home from school,
none of them know.
I tried to lock David in his room,
to punch Walter away from that door.
To save them.

I could wait
until the sun moves just so,
until the chink of light
hits the face.
Then I would see
who it is.
I'd be ready.

No

January 1957
Cromwell, Connecticut

Thelma says I must go
with these men. One is tall and lank, his eyes flitting
all over me. Thelma says I must go.
The other is shorter, his eyes steady. Thelma
leaves the room. I could
run like a girl over plowed fields to the bridge.
One lays his hand on my shoulder. Too close.
No. The word is small. I shout it, but
I have no voice.
Squirm away. No.
Thelma is gone. These two have plenty
to say, soft and lulling. No:
shaped in air and fallen to the floor. Cold spot on my arm, hot
prick like a snake. Short one says
sit down.
I have no daughter. Hot.
Hit the tall one. The small one
close. Both. Room is gray. Breathing.
Thelma. Arms.
Bed on wheels. Someone
sick. Me.
Lie down.
Arms
tied
to my stomach. Eyes, mouth.
Screaming.

Against My Dreams

This Place

January 1957
Connecticut Valley State Hospital, Middletown, Connecticut

It's cold in here.
"Take your medicine,"
this one says, and he
does not smile.
Here there is only
the slow tick.
Bread. Sleep. Tick
tock. That one who looks like
Thelma sits on my bed, her face
not moving.
"How are you, Mother?" How
does she think I am? Slick
green hallways, glaring
lights. "The children are
fine," she says, so
smilingly. My feet don't
make any sound. "Take
your medicine." I follow them
around, these silent feet. Tick
tock. That clock's
big face is in every
room. A darkness
seeps
from under
my bed, a thin shadow
joining with the night.
The night
hulks
after me.
I feel its hot
breath
on my skin.
It used to be

a dimness
under my walking
feet. Behind
me nothing
but that dimness
at first. When things began to slow
down, I could sense
its press. It
deepened, grew
until it breathed, moved
of its own
will. The morning
light fades and I can't
see, remember.
I slide. Suddenly
nothing, a cliff
and I've jumped.

Wind

May 1957
Mark Twain Arms Rest Home, Hartford, Connecticut

Everything flies up, whirls, touches down,
        but the wind does not cease, so everything
flies up again. Nothing ever really settles.
        I must rise and run about to gather my clothes.
The furniture whirls, too, shuddering, all but
        this big bed where I can lie still and catch
my breath. Even the rug flaps, its red flowers
        tossing their heads, stems rippling. The lamp,
the table, the chair, the dresser all shiver and rock
        in the gale. It carries no good with it.

Most of the time I try not to think, but the wind rustles
        the thoughts from my head, sets them spinning
around the room. Some days I fling the covers off,
        curse the wind, and think whatever I like. Often
it's best to stay in bed, to make myself small and flat,
        let the wind meet no resistance.

Below the rug, below the floor, below the house
        lie the great Beast's deep footprints, full
of dark water beaten by the squall into froth.
        The Beast loves the wind, its own breath.
Cold air and hot breath rush over me at once,
        so I can never tell them apart.

Once in a while I pin on my hat, walk down the stairs
        to the street. The breeze is calm then, and I
hardly look over my shoulder to see if the Beast
        follows. But it waits in my room with the wind,
holding its breath until I come back. When I open the door,
        it rises, blasts with a roar through the narrow
hall. I press my hat against my head, but the storm
        takes it anyway, hatpin and all. Such a fierce blow
that all my careful pinning comes undone, my hair flies wild.
        Right off my scalp it flies, like milkweed puff.

Against My Dreams

Taking Up Space

September 1962
Mark Twain Arms Rest Home, Hartford, Connecticut

They go through my things.
They open the drawers, look in my closet, touch
my dresses, my sweater, their nosy fingers
on my underwear. Precious things
under my bed—my letters
to God, my blue leather shoes—
I cannot bear their hands on those.
They dare not come around
at night when I sit guard, waiting
for their long noses, holding
my purse in my lap. But in the day
when I go to eat boiled food, I have
no lock and key.
In winter we all slept
in the kitchen, Papa, Mama, the boys, the girls,
and me. In summer we all slept
in the mountain *seter*, one room softened
by hay, the cows munching new grass
outside. Andrew and I slept
in the same bed until he began taking up space
with his rheumy eyes and whiskey breath.
These women with their busybody noses and fingers
talk to me, but I keep to my own
thoughts. I don't want
their words rattling inside my head
when I need to think clearly.

A Tooth in God's Chair

October 1968
Mark Twain Arms Rest Home, Hartford, Connecticut

Why are these faces at my dinner table?
They smack their lips, thieve each other's
bread, cut the napkins with their knives.
Someone keeps stealing my money.
I hold my purse with both hands.
That one with whiskers begs cigarettes.

Thelma doesn't come. David and Linda
are stiff as sticks, their young faces odd
against this swarm. I tell them don't listen to
the Lawyers, the Roman Catholics, the Beast.
It's a sin to whistle when money is involved.
I could pack my bags, go home with them.

The righteous shall inherit the earth.
That's what Oral Roberts says on the TV.
I could slip through the crack beneath
the window, fly to the clouds. I could rain
over the earth the water that gives life.
I could buy the house next to Thelma's.

Long Ago Room

August 1980
Mark Twain Arms Rest Home, Hartford, Connecticut

Bed under the window, dresser, closet door,
blue roses on the wallpaper. In the mirror
another room where blue roses are made
tiny, the bed and its window grown small.

My hat with its pearl hatpin roosts like a crow
on the corner of the bed, as if it belongs.
I perch in this wooden rocker, afraid
to move too much, a slight rocking back
and forth, arriving forever a stranger.

I'll see what night brings, perhaps
even rest. The cuckoo clock downstairs
keeps singing. If you take your clothes off
three times under the tree where
a cuckoo calls, you'll get three wishes.

Rocking back and forth, rocking back to
smoke from the open fireplace, the sun
out most of the night. I'd forgotten
hay draped over fences to dry, milk shooting
hard from an udder, currants growing
in Mama's garden. The schoolmaster
arrived like a turtle, his books upon his back.

I run, my hair flying over my shoulders,
weave a crown of day-and-nights, their petals
yellow and purple jewels against my hair's
darkness. In the mirror a smaller room, small
bed, small blue roses, a small me, rocking.

Author's Note

When I was a little girl, it was always a big event when my grandmother came to visit. My other grandparents had died before I was born, so Nana was the only grandparent I knew. During her weekend visits she'd cook Old Country foods, she'd crochet and knit amazingly detailed pieces, and she'd speak with her lilting accent, drawing a quick in-breath at the beginnings of her sentences. Since my mother worked, Nana would help with the household chores, and I'd follow her outside to the clothesline and later watch as she sprinkled the clothes and pillowcases to ready them for the iron. We didn't have a spare bedroom, so my parents fixed up a space in the attic, and I'd sleep with Nana there. She'd tell me a story or we'd count together in Norwegian, and in the morning I'd linger while she captured her long white hair into a neat bun. To this day, when I hear the sound of rain on the roof, I can feel the comfort and warmth of my grandmother.

When I was about eight years old, something changed drastically, though I didn't understand what it was. One day while Nana was visiting, my mother asked me to go to our neighbor's house to play. But Mom's well-laid plans went awry, and I came home in the middle of a strange scene: Two men dressed in white were trying to coax my grandmother into leaving with them, and it was clear that she didn't want to go. My mother told me to wait in our basement playroom, where I continued to hear the sounds of Nana's distress. After an endless number of weeks, Nana returned, but she wasn't the grandmother I'd always known.

I've long felt a need to reclaim the important place my grandmother held in my early life, to explain her mental illness to myself, and to see her as a whole and vibrant human being. When I was near the end of my graduate program and living in New York City, I found myself writing a poem in her voice and was encouraged to continue by my favorite professor and mentor, James Merritt.

Before long, I was deep into research about Norwegian traditions, mythology, and folktales and about the history of Norwegian immigration and the experiences of immigrants. I read every book I could get my hands on, discovering the richness of Norwegian literature, including the novels of Nobel Prize winners Sigrid Undset and Knut Hamsun, which contain a vast array of Norwegian characters and voices.

Eventually research wasn't enough—I needed to see where my grandmother came from—and I traveled to Norway, where I met my cousins, who hosted me in their homes, lavishly fed me, and told me stories that brought family history to life. My cousin Kari took me to the farms where my grandmother and great grandmother were born; the church in Åseral where my grandmother was confirmed; the churchyard where her parents and younger sister were buried, alongside the graves of RAF pilots and crew members lost there during World War II; the tiny schoolhouse where my grandmother had her brief education; and the remnants of the farmhouse my great-great grandfather built. My cousin Nora and her husband Reidar took me to a cultural festival in Åseral, where I learned about local traditional crafts, dress, customs, and foods. My cousin Else Marie baked me the most glorious cakes, and both she and my cousin Gudrun sparkled as we attempted to bridge our language difficulties. My cousin Olav, a champion accordion player, shared his music, and his thirteen-year-old son Frank accompanied me on countless country walks. I met my cousins' children and their children. One of the most emotional moments of my visit was when my cousins presented me with a pin that had belonged to my great grandmother, enamel on copper depicting a single red rose. As I learned about my grandmother's beginnings in the good company of my Norwegian family, I came to understand more about her and about who I am.

I also traveled in southern Norway on my own, visiting museums and researching emigration records. Norway lost more than a third of its population to emigration, and it is said that there are more people of Norwegian descent in America than there are in Norway. Everywhere I went gracious Norwegians shared their enthusiasm about meeting an American in search of her roots.

Until I went to Norway and heard family stories beyond the ones my mother had told me, I didn't know that in her childhood my grandmother had lost her little sister to tuberculosis. That startling discovery was the seed for the first poem in the collection, "Without God." Walking where Nana had walked and seeing what she'd seen when she was a girl enabled me to create images for these poems that I couldn't have invented otherwise. All that I learned from my Norwegian family and from visits to museums in Norway is woven throughout the collection. For example, in one museum I saw a chair made from a thick log. A section was cut from it to leave a backrest and seat, which were smoothed and varnished. The outside of the chair remained covered by bark. A half-circle of human teeth had been pounded into the seat's outer edge, and when the guide told me the folk belief behind that odd decorative practice, it became the core of the poem entitled, "Stranger," and gave me the title, "A Tooth in God's Chair."

Back in New York, I searched photographic archives and wandered Manhattan's Upper West Side, where my grandmother worked as a live-in maid upon her arrival. In the New-York Historical Society's collection I noticed a photograph of a huge, ornate walk-in linen closet, which inspired the imagined scene when my grandmother associates the avalanche that had crushed a farm in her village—a story my cousins had told me—with her paralyzing loneliness and longing for home. I can't imagine what it took for my young grandmother to adjust to New York

City. Roaming the neighborhoods of the Upper West Side, I encountered the statues of Joan of Arc and of Mary conquering the snake, which provided images for "Woman of Metal" and "The Beast," two poems in which she's trying to make sense of her surroundings. In researching immigrant experiences of being processed at Ellis Island, I learned that when the buildings there were being restored, workers discovered graffiti on many of the outside walls—people wrote their real names there, the names that had been Americanized and lost. That fact gave me the focus for the poem called "Ellis Island," the place where my grandmother, too, lost her name.

Another gift from my Norwegian trip was meeting the man who would become my husband, an American wildlife biologist who'd been doing a whale survey north of Norway in the Barents Sea. A serendipitous series of events led to our crossing paths. When we married a year later, I left New York for the Pacific Northwest, because writers can live anywhere, but sea otters don't. Though I know it doesn't compare to my grandmother's experience, my dislocation from everything and everyone I'd known gave me a tiny glimpse into what she might have felt when she emigrated. I visited the Nordic Heritage Museum in Seattle and interviewed her contemporaries at the Norse Home. I also kept a journal in her voice for a year, the source of most of the poems in this collection. When my husband and I traveled to Norway together a few years later, we visited my cousins and then explored southern Norway, eventually taking an overnight ferry to Denmark. Like my grandmother had done eighty years earlier, I watched Norway slip out of sight over the horizon.

Against My Dreams

About The Author

Linda Strever grew up in Connecticut and earned a B.S. in English Education at Central Connecticut State University. In her mid-thirties she moved to Brooklyn, New York, earning an MFA in Creative Writing at Brooklyn College, City University of New York, where she was awarded the Louis Goodman  Creative Writing Scholarship. Her poetry credits include *Crab Creek Review; Floating Bridge Review; Spoon River Poetry Review; CALYX, a Journal of Art and Literature by Women; Beloit Poetry Journal; Nimrod: International Journal of Prose and Poetry; Adanna* and others.

Winner of the Lois Cranston Memorial Poetry Prize from *CALYX Journal*, her work has been a finalist for the *Spoon River Poetry Review* Editors' Prize, the *Crab Creek Review* Poetry Award, the Eludia Award for Fiction, and the A. E. Coppard Prize for Fiction, as well as in the William Van Wert Fiction Competition and the Summer Literary Seminars Fiction Competition.

Against My Dreams was a finalist for both the Intro Series Poetry Prize and the Levis Poetry Prize from Four-Way Books, the New Issues Press Award in Poetry, and the Ohio State University Press Award in Poetry.

She has worked as a proofreader, editor, graphic artist, teacher, trainer, and mediator and lives with her husband in the Pacific Northwest.

photo © Barry Troutman